th
is always
greener

the grass is always greener

rural life and Christian faith

CHURCH HOUSE
PUBLISHING

Church House Publishing
Church House
Great Smith Street
London
SW1P 3NZ

ISBN 0 7151 5547 4

Board of Mission Occasional Paper
No. 11

Published 2002 for the Board
of Mission of the Archbishops'
Council by Church House Publishing

*Copyright © The Archbishops' Council
2002*

Cover illustration by Leigh Hurlock

Typeset in 10/11 Franklin Gothic

Printed by Halstan & Co. Ltd,
Amersham, Bucks

*This report has only the authority of
the committee who produced it. It
has been approved by the Board of
Mission of the Archbishops' Council.*

contents

preface

'One of the powerful images which we have of the English countryside is that it is an idyllic "world apart", a place which is isolated and insulated from the rest of the hectic, urban-centred world.' So said the important report of the Archbishops' Commission on Rural Areas, *Faith in the Countryside*, published in 1990. Ten years on, with the aftermath of BSE, a great upheaval in agriculture and the foot-and-mouth crisis, such a rosy picture is not nearly as widespread. Yet misperceptions and misunderstandings about life in the countryside remain. This is in spite of the fact that about seventy per cent of people who live in rural communities today are first generation villagers who have either moved there in their lifetime or are the first of their family to be born in that situation.

Britain today is an increasingly urban society, with more and more people living in towns and cities. Yet you only have to look at a map of Britain to see just how large an area may still be characterized as rural. So, how do rural and urban relate to one another? What is the reality of rural life? And what is the role of the Church within it? Amid all the changes affecting rural life, the Church continues to have strong presence, making a significant contribution to so many rural communities. Its buildings can provide a village with its praying heart, a centre for the celebration of its joys and the marking of its grief, and a focus for friendship and pastoral care. Its members are deeply involved in the issues affecting the countryside today and they are themselves affected by them.

This short study guide is not a course as such but a resource, which may be used in a variety of different ways. Here you will find real stories of real people, intended to help local church groups – whether in a city, a town or a village – to explore and better understand some of the issues facing rural areas and the rural church today.

✠ Michael Exon:
Chairman, Rural Affairs Committee of the Board of Mission

acknowledgements

I am grateful to the members of the Rural Affairs Committee for their interest in theological reflection on rural issues which led to the production of the material for this book, and for their support and encouragement throughout.

I am especially grateful to the Revd Canon Jeremy Martineau and to Mrs Margaret Cosh for providing me with extra material.

Dr Anne Richards
Mission Theology Adviser
The Archbishops' Council

acknowledgments

introduction

This little book of stories is intended for everyone who is interested in our rural life. That does not mean that only people living in the countryside can use it. All of us have some connection with rurality, whether it's because we live or work there, because we take holidays or make visits to the countryside, or because we purchase and consume products that come from rural food producers.

Yet there are many differing perceptions of what rural life is like. One reason why the book is called *the grass is always greener* is because for many people the countryside does indeed seem to have a more peaceful, more idyllic lifestyle. However, when they come to experience it fully, they find the realities of rural life come as a shock. Conversely, some people in the countryside have differing views of urban living and of the attitudes of city folk towards their lives, sports and livelihoods. The stories in each of the sections of this book try to provide a way to look at these perceptions and attitudes. They can then be used to look more closely and thoughtfully at what help and support the local church can give. They can form the basis of Advent or Lent reflections, for study or house groups, or indeed for any kind of fellowship of lay and ordained people who want to think, pray and study together about rural issues.

The stories represent a selection drawn from the many known to us. We chose them for the resonance they may have for as wide a group of readers as possible. Yet since we began drawing the stories together, life in the countryside has been changed for ever. Foot-and-mouth disease, arriving on the back of the BSE crisis, has changed the context of all our thoughts, prayers and theological reflection and highlighted the role of the local church as a source of support and help. As we looked at the stories again, we realized how many of them had farmers or farming somewhere in their background, even if these were not the main thrust of the narrative. We could have overwhelmed the book with farming stories of the fear, misery and despair that have become known to us, but that would have distorted our intention to invite reflection on many deep issues in the countryside. Instead we have focused on one story of the very many, a story that speaks to us of *hope*. In this way, we would like to look beyond the terrible events that have overtaken our country life and reach out to a God who calls us always to be partners in the renewal of the creation, a God who has taught us in Christ that new life is within our grasp.

chapter 1
food

Aim: to look at the contrast between the realities of food production and the idea that food comes from shops and especially supermarkets

story

Amanda, aged twelve, needed medical help when she lost a great deal of weight very quickly after she had begun to refuse food. She claimed she was now vegan and could not eat a very large number of common foods. Although it was first thought she was suffering from the eating disorder anorexia nervosa, her doctor found that her problems had begun when she had discovered that food was not, in fact, synthetic. A city dweller, she had only ever shopped with her mother in a local supermarket, buying food largely in tins and packets. Her only exposure to live animals had been through pets and a children's zoo. She had never visited a butcher's shop or eaten offal. She had learned that 'milk comes from cows' from books for small children, but regarded this as entirely mythical.

On discovering that the meat she had been eating was the flesh of animals, that dairy products come from cows, that eggs come from chickens and that animals are raised and slaughtered for food, she became revolted by the idea of eating. She had become unable to cope with eating on two counts: that much food is not made of 'clean' synthetic materials, but from messy animal parts; and that sweet, cuddly animals are killed for human beings to eat.

discussion

Amanda's story demonstrates some important aspects of life in our own contemporary western society. For many people eating their food every day, consumption of the food may be divorced from the realities of its production. The processing and presentation of food often have no immediate link to its origin, and foods may be coloured or shaped beyond their natural appearance to attract the customer. Food advertising often concentrates on this kind of presentation, combining attractiveness of packaging and taste with information about its calorific content for the weight-conscious. Where the advertising alludes to the freshness of food, the portrayal of origins may be an idyllic farm setting or pictures of cartoon animals. People whose attitudes are conditioned and shaped by these images and experiences of the food they buy, who have no direct experience of the farming life of the countryside, may find it more difficult to reconcile the realities of food production with how they buy and consume the produce.

Further, many urban dwellers do not need to be aware of the seasonal cycle of meat and vegetable production, since most foods are now available in the larger supermarkets all year round. The only thing the consumer may be aware of is variation in the price of strawberries, although some celebrity chefs (such as Delia Smith) have drawn attention to the loss of taste quality in some imported foods.

Another question we have to ask ourselves is about some popular presentations of animals. Television programmes focusing on vets such as *All Creatures Great and Small, Vets in Practice* and *Animal Hospital* (which have high popularity ratings) may often have sentimental perspectives on saving animals (with corresponding distress when animals die). This may make it more difficult for people to set this against the realities of producing animals for food. Many people may never have seen an animal being born or seen an animal die and find some rural attitudes towards animals unbearably robust, or even barbaric. For example, some holidaymakers have been known to give up a 'learn to fish' outing on the first day when faced with hooks, flies and live bait.

Theologically, the Church has problems in presenting a clear and robust creation theology that addresses all these complex issues. We need to articulate a deeper theological understanding of why we are a created human species having particular nutritional needs for healthy bodies. We also need to look at what it means to be at the top of the food chain without natural

predators of our own and at what influence the domestication
of animals for food use and the history of agriculture have had
both in human history and in the history of the planet. The need
to consume food is deeply embedded in our theology and in our
religious experience. We have also traditionally drawn an
analogy between right relationship with God and the idea of
being fed. The desire to be fed is rooted in the Lord's Prayer
and is at the heart of both voluntary fasting as a religious
discipline and thanksgiving before meals. The loss of such
religious observance in households therefore means that many
of us are not reminded of the link between God's providence
and the created order each time we eat our food.

In today's western society the richer populations have choices
about food use, in stark contrast to much of the rest of the
globe. We can afford to roast or grill away the fat and throw
away skin and bones. In other societies such profligate waste
of an animal's resources is unthinkable. We may no longer
appreciate the theological edge derived from the experience
of hunger, or fasting, nor appreciate the notion of harvest or of
abundance. This may have the result of reducing much biblical
imagery and metaphor to mere ideas about common sharing
and fellowship. Further, the pragmatic outworking is to see the
plight of farmers as unrelated to the experience of ordinary life.
This means that the place of farmers and other food producers
needs to be highlighted as crucial to particular kinds of
theological insights. In the light of this, what place should we
give to 'animal theology'? Is it crucial to a theological way
forward or is it simply a luxury we can now afford? We need
to be clearer about what we can say about animals in the
stewardship of the whole created order.

some suggestions for Bible study

Genesis 1.26

Leviticus 11

Matthew 15.16-20

Acts 10.9-16

questions for discussion

- What do you think animals are for?
- Do you care about what happens when animals die? If so, why? What might be unacceptable to you about how or why animals die?
- Are you vegetarian/vegan? Why?
- Are there particular foods you won't eat? Why? What alternatives are acceptable to you?
- Could you slaughter, prepare and cook animal food if you had to? If not, why not?

possibilities for drama or role play

Can you sympathize with what happened to Amanda? What would you have done if you were her parents? What would you have advised if you were her doctor? What do you think might have happened to her?

Look at advertising for food. Imagine you had to promote or endorse a product. What words would you use? What might make people buy? Why?

reflection

How does God want us to behave in respect of animals? How does this affect how we think about farmers and farming, other food producers, food promoters and sellers, supermarkets and local shops?

a hymn and a prayer

For example: 'Guide me, O thou great Redeemer'[1] or 'We come as guests invited'[2]

God,

you blessed and broke bread for your friends to share with you:

share your love with us always, as we seek to share your love with others.

Amen.

chapter 2
dark

Aim: to examine the contrast between perceptions of a rural idyll and the reality of life in the countryside

story

Florence, who had lived all her life in London, went to visit her sister who had recently moved to a remote rural location. She painted the forthcoming visit to her friends in terms of an idyllic setting that was everything the city was not. It was peaceful, while the city was noisy. It was clean, while the city was dirty. It was slow-moving while the city was busy. It was a nurturing, soothing environment for the stressed-out. In short, it was everything one might envisage for a 'dream' holiday – a pastoral paradise.

When Florence arrived (bearing gifts of eggs 'fresh from the country'), she discovered that the reality was very different. The first difficulty she encountered was darkness. She had never lived in a situation where, at night, it was pitch dark and she could not move around easily. She found the dark unnerving, the more so because the local people did not seem to have a problem getting around without proper pavements or street lighting.[1] She realized that she was dependent on reflected light to make her feel safe and found the absence of headlights passing the house a deep and unnerving loss.

Her next problem was that the rural location to which her sister had moved turned out to be anything but peaceful. The adjoining farm created all kinds of noise: the church clock set off dogs barking, cockerels crowed and animals in the fields made much louder noises than expected. She found that birds drove her mad. Where she found aircraft and traffic noise could be reduced to a background she could filter out, she found unexpected and erratic rural noise impossible to ignore.

Her ideas of a 'clean' environment were also shattered. She had come unprepared for mud and had no appropriate footwear or clothing. Debris from agricultural work and hedge cutting got in her hair. She also became obsessed by worries about mice and insects as erratic and uncontrollable elements in her previously ordered and sanitized life. She found that the people in the tiny village were not able to spend long periods over the garden gate passing the time of day, but were busy with their own lives and did not necessarily live more slowly. Moreover, some of the people in the remote location were struggling in as much poverty as people she had encountered in deprived parts of the city.

Disillusioned, Florence went home and decided to take a holiday next time in a decent hotel somewhere by the sea.

discussion

Florence's story illustrates some of the problems of perception that can occur when people idealize notions of the countryside and of rural life. Such distorted perceptions can, of course, occur in both directions and people from rural areas may also have unrealistic ideas about urban life. There is, however, a mythic dimension to the notion of the rural idyll, bolstered by television images of countryside locations in which the sun always shines and peace is always to be found. People may adopt a 'National Trust' view of country life, in which the countryside is both contained and beautifully presented and somehow 'kept' as a treasure for visitors. 'Pretty villages' and 'pretty churches' therefore become consumable items for visitors and tourists and, while there may be some benefit from this, other problems of perception may become more acute. Visitors may have few ideas about how to behave on farmland – where to walk or to park, or how to control their dogs, and may have little idea that the countryside is a place where people also work and worship. People may also be disappointed when their 'pretty church' turns out to be cold and draughty, without a full range of services staffed by a permanent incumbent, and not in possession of a peal of bells or large choir for their dream wedding.

Although much language from the Bible draws on the experience of life lived in an isolated, dark, unpopulated and agricultural setting, and Jesus himself practised an itinerant ministry, much of our modern theology derives from a Jesus in Jerusalem and the spread of the gospel to major urban centres. Similarly, much of our sophisticated western theology seems to assume that we grow up with God in an urban environment as well as looking to an eschatological model of the heavenly city in which God is governor. This is in spite of the fact that much of the global population still lives and witnesses to God in rural situations and whose experience of living the Christian faith is shaped in those environments. For us, whether we realize it or not, the experience of living in the city has had a powerful effect on shaping the kind of language we use. When, as Christians, we spend time looking at the modes of engagement between the Church and the world, we often envision the world of the metropolis. In this world, secular processes present challenges for the Church's mission. This is the world of urban church planting, of the identification of under-churched areas, of engagement with issues of marginalization and social justice, but often without considering the analogous problems faced by the Church in the countryside. How do we address the very real mission questions that surround keeping the faith alive in small villages, many depressed by lack of housing and work and by the farming crises? The idea of the retreat, for some people, has connotations and expectations of the rural idyll: a place of peace and refreshment in a different setting where we can recharge batteries before returning to the challenges of Christian witness in difficult urban and suburban environments. This similarly deflects attention from the real needs of Christian witness in the countryside that should be included in our theological conversations and priorities.

suggestions for Bible study

Psalm 23

Isaiah 9.2-7

Revelation 21.1-4, 22-27

questions for discussion

- Have you ever taken a holiday where the place was entirely unlike what you expected? If so, what did you do?
- If you go for a 'day out in the city' or a 'day out in the country' where do you go and why? Where would you *not* go, and why?
- Do you know how to behave in the countryside, if you are a) a day tripper on a coach tour, b) a walker, c) a dog owner? What would make you 'streetwise' in the city?

possibilities for drama or role play

How might Florence explain how she felt to her sister? What would her sister say?

How would Florence react when she got home; how would she tell the story to her family?

What would happen if the 'country' sister visited the 'city' sister?

Imagine that you went on a holiday that proved quite different to expectations. What would you say to the tour guide about what you expected and what you actually experienced?

reflection

What does God expect of us when we encounter the strange and the unfamiliar?

How can such encounters help equip us to be better witnesses or missionaries?

a hymn and a prayer

For example: 'Lead, kindly Light'[2] or 'Like a candle flame'[3]

God,

you are the light of the world, you are the peace we yearn and long for:

help us to live in your light and share your peace.

Amen.

chapter 3
pub

Aim: to examine the contrast between those whose lives and work are traditionally rooted in one place and those who commute

story

Jon, who lives in a rural village, but stays up in London during the week, was sitting in his local pub talking to some other people from the village. He was recounting stories of his close relationships with work colleagues and their plans to celebrate the Millennium by flying to South America for the party of a lifetime. For Jon, to whom travel is easy, accessible and necessary, life is impoverished if people do not network with others, explore other places and move from one location to another.

Jon then got into an argument with Danny, a young farm worker who had been born and brought up in the village, who had always worked there, and who had never travelled very far from his home. Jon argued that Danny's life was blinkered and insubstantial. He suggested that the rich, vibrant, ever-changing flow of city life, work life and having networks of other people for perpetual variety was what made life worth living. Danny argued that the depth of relationship afforded by commitment to one place and to its people, and to the communal life of the village was more important than Jon's frothy, fast-moving existence. He felt that Jon had just pushed into village life, taking what he wanted and consuming the village's goods and services without giving anything back. Jon was absent more often than present and therefore not a contributor to the community except of an irrelevant fantasy life of other places and unknown people. Danny said 'we care about our own: you care about yourself'. Jon, a forceful and articulate man, argued back that people like Danny were dinosaurs, part of a non-contributing backwater. He said Danny represented a reactionary and traditionalist set of people out of touch with the realities of modern living and claimed that in a few years the entire village would be owned by people like him. The dispute festered in the village, with Danny's mates seeing Jon's attitude as a direct attack on their values and their way of life. A week later, Jon's house was vandalized.

discussion

Changes affecting the whole of western society may come to different geographical areas of the country at different rates. One very large change is the availability of travel options and the fluid ability of people to move between their places of home and work. Commuter options are so widespread that people may travel to major city centres from quite rural locations, or they may work sometimes from home, networking to business centres and work contacts. The effect of this is to divide people's lives into a series of important networks, of which 'home' or the place where they usually live, may be only one part. For those who have lived and worked in one place for many years and who are instrumental in building up and sustaining the community, engagement with people who live their lives in different locations may be challenging. They may only be interested in a 'second home' from which they are largely absent. It can make it difficult for faithful members of a congregation to see clearly what contribution commuters make to the life of the local church. Sometimes there are possibilities for enrichment of the community, but also for demoralization and damage. Much depends on arbitrary labelling of people, such as commuters, as 'insiders' going out or 'outsiders' coming in. There are also questions of conflict resolution between opposing views. What kind of people have the ability to be reconcilers or peacemakers in situations like this?

The Bible contains many examples of different kinds of communities working out whether the best strategy is conflict, absorption or peaceful readjustment. Jesus, too, asks for a hard look at what we think we mean by 'neighbours' and the need for us to befriend and seek to understand the strangers in our midst. It is an important mission question what kinds of accommodation can properly exist between the incursion of commuters into traditional 'rooted' communities and what part the life of the local church may have in this. Does the rooted community in fact have a depth of communal life that provides spiritual nourishment to people forced to spread themselves between the home and the work community? Where new developments are built near to existing villages, questions of mission strategy for the integration of the whole church community may become especially acute and may require particular pastoral sensitivity. Perhaps commuters working long hours and exhausted by travel do not need to be asked to shoulder more burdens from the local church, but perhaps they need secure and reliable childcare and support from their neighbours? Perhaps commuters bring new and refreshing ideas from other experiences in their lives that can inspire a rooted community?

some ideas for Bible study

2 Kings 5

Luke 16.19-31

Luke 15.11-end

questions for discussion

- If you won the lottery would you buy a house in the country, or a flat in a city? Give reasons for your choice.
- If you stay at home most of the day, do you wish you could go to other places? Say why or why not. What do you think about commuters or jet-setters?
- If you commute to work, do you wish you could stay at home? Say why or why not.
- What do you think about housewives/ househusbands or people who work from home?
- Do you think this story is mainly about money? Say why or why not.

possibilities for drama or role play

Go over the story as Jon and Danny. What difference would it make if the characters were called Joanne and Sally or if the two protagonists were from different ethnic backgrounds?

What do you think Jon felt when his house was vandalized? What would he tell the police? What would he say to Danny next time he saw him? What would Danny say?

reflection

How do you think God expects us to behave towards our neighbours? What makes us good neighbours? How does thinking about neighbours help us to be better witnesses to Christ?

a hymn and a prayer

For example: 'City of God, how broad and far',[1] or 'Jesus put this song into our hearts'[2]

> God,
>
> you go with us in all our travels; you are the stranger on the Emmaus Road,
>
> and yet at home you wait for us, your arms open in welcome.
>
> Help us to meet you everywhere we go.
>
> Amen.

chapter 4

grave

Aim: to examine the contrast between the continuous history of generations and its effect on community, and the influx of others whose histories lie elsewhere

story

A committed church-going couple, Tim and Roma, who were possessed of considerable personal success and wealth, bought a large house in a tiny, rural village. They immediately devoted themselves to the local church, and became major contributors to its financial resources. They then quickly became frustrated when they discovered that all decisions tended to be filtered from the small church council through the mind of one very elderly churchgoer, Cecil, who took a very long time to pronounce his view on any matter. Tim and Roma, who were supporting the church with a great deal of money, really felt that their commitment should count for something and wanted to have their views given more weight in the decision-making process. In particular, they had strong feelings about the reordering of the church to be more family friendly and about the use of more modern kinds of worship. They discovered a general resistance to their ideas of what the church could be like, coupled with a quiet refusal to discuss some ideas as non-negotiable issues. There did not, however, seem to be any such qualms about asking Tim and Roma for more money. Unused to this way of doing things and these kinds of attitudes, they began to challenge the habit of referring everything to Cecil's generally conservative opinion as if this settled the argument. This generated hostility among other members of the congregation until Tim and Roma wondered if they should leave and find another church.

Eventually, one of the most senior church members took them out to the churchyard and pointed out the rows of ancient headstones belonging to generations of Cecil's family. In that village, churchgoers came from families who had grown up with, died alongside, and intermarried with, members of Cecil's family. Their histories were bound up with his, until he had become incontrovertibly associated with the life and health of the church. Cecil took a long time over decisions because he tended to think deeply about the consequences of those decisions for the entire community of people, and the rest of the congregation trusted him. A point was made to the couple that they were not unwelcome in the local church, nor were their views deemed unworthy or trivial. The difficulty was that the new couple were felt to be caught up in a contemporary notion of church which was different every Sunday and therefore cut off from long-standing tradition. Tim and Roma couldn't yet belong to the long history of prayer and worship in that place on which the church and local village life was based: 'you might as well be Americans'.

discussion

The theologian Walter Wink, in his Powers trilogy[1], argues that the 'angel' or spiritual personality of a church can only be understood by proper attention to both a current 'snapshot' of what is happening at the present moment, and a much longer view of the history of the place. The present situation matters, but so do the life-stories that have, over time, been played out in history. Both perspectives are needed to make an accurate and sensitive assessment of what God has been doing in the life of the church and what the possibilities are for the ongoing and future life of the village community. In this story, the two perspectives clashed rather than integrated, causing difficulties on both sides. If each church has its 'angel', then the histories of worshipping communities do make a significant difference to the life of the church, but this has to be seen as a liberating influence and not as a trap. What is important is that the interaction between the two perspectives should be an open and creative process and not hindered by secrecy or by the assumption that everyone somehow knows how things are done. This is particularly true for a new minister entering a new situation, who may be unfairly expected to have an intuitive understanding of the traditional functioning of the church. Similarly, change in the church, outreach and witness to the wider community have to emerge from a general willingness to be inclusive and welcoming. This is despite the fact that outside influences may bring challenge and what feels like dangerous change.

some ideas for Bible study

Wisdom 7.15-22

Ecclesiastes 5.1-7

Luke 9.28-36

questions for discussion:

- Have you come across villages where 'the ancient traditions' or 'old ways of doing things' remain important? If yes, what were the circumstances?
- Why might it be important to learn as much as possible about the history of a place before attempting to change anything?
- Do you think change is always for the better? If so, why? If not, why not?

possibilities for drama or role play

Try being Tim and Roma discussing new ideas for worship with members of the church council. Where would the question of money come into all this?

How would Cecil explain his understanding of responsibility?

How could church people make Tim and Roma feel really welcome and valued?

reflection

If it is a missionary task to seek to understand the 'angel' of a place, then this requires a sensitive 'mission audit' to include not just what is going on in a local church, but what brought it to be that way. What history of Christian witness has been inherited by the present congregation, or what problems and difficulties have arisen and perhaps never been properly resolved?

a hymn and a prayer

For example: 'God is working his purpose out as year succeeds to year',[2] or 'How lovely is thy dwelling-place, O Lord of hosts'[3]

> God,
>
> you hold all history in your hands;
>
> all time is yours and all eternity.
>
> Help us to look beyond the small demands
> of our anxious present
>
> and catch a glimpse of our everlasting home.
>
> Amen.

chapter 5
fish

*Aim: to examine the contrast between global questions
of renewing and sustaining the earth and more local,
countryside issues*

story

A group of young people from a sixth form college was required
to work on a project on environmental issues. These young people
had spent time learning about global warming, environmental
pollution, the depletion of the rain forests and other natural
reserves, exploitation of animal populations, and overuse
of fossil fuels. All of them were aware of the importance of
recycling, conservation and resource management. Some,
but not all, came from the Christian tradition.

In pursuing the project, the students were asked to study the
global question through a field trip to a rural environment in
which these issues were being addressed. Problems ensued
when one pair of students, Martha and Colm, pursued their
enquiry in a small fishing village. Simple ideas about the evils
of overfishing and stock management quickly became
complicated by what they learned about competition from
foreign fishing fleets, EU regulations regarding fish harvests
and the struggle for an adequate livelihood in the face of
financial and market controls. As the young people learned
more about the danger and difficulty of coping with the
environment, they found their sympathy for the fishermen's
work conflicting with their idealism and wider view of a global
picture. Evidence that people were bending rules in order to
survive, also made it very difficult for them to reconcile their
global vision with the day-to-day realities of earning a living and
supporting families. This was especially true where the village
was also involved in communally helping and sustaining families
in which there had been fatalities at sea. Martha and Colm
investigated how people could turn their hands to other kinds of
business, but although there was some evidence for this, most

of the people they talked to mentioned a fragile infrastructure entirely dependent on shared help. Branching out took workers away from what was left of the industry and made it ever more difficult to sustain it as a major part of village life and culture, which had otherwise kept going for generations and was commemorated in the monuments and windows of the largest local church. The village people were especially bitter that their small community was unlikely to survive competition from larger and better equipped fishing enterprises and that much of their spirit and life would end up as photographs and mementoes in a village museum.

Martha and Colm found it extremely difficult to apply their experience to their learned philosophy and began to see the process of writing up their project as hopeless. The people in the fishing community felt extremely distant from London and the EU, never mind the rest of the world. What they did know about was the local fishing environment, about the seasonal cycles for the catch, the relation of the catch to the local food chain, the effects of pollutants on fish and the effects of weather. They were extremely concerned for the effective management and preservation of the fishing environment and the place of human beings in that web of relationships. They were very concerned about those only interested in exploitation and the manipulators of regulations and felt very depressed and cynical that they were always the last to be consulted, if consulted at all. Martha and Colm wrote up their project to reflect these attitudes and at assessment were asked to consider whether their experiences represented 'an unusual case'.

discussion

One of the marks of mission states explicitly that we must strive to maintain the integrity of creation and to sustain and renew the earth. This fits with a mission theological view that the creator God invites us to be partners in the creation by assuming responsibility for stewardship of the earth's resources. Further, we are committed to limiting and repairing damage to the planet of which we are integrally a part. Our responsibility includes identifying the damage already done, understanding its consequences and finding ways of ensuring further damage does not occur.

Unfortunately the realities of daily life may mean that this becomes an idealistic luxury for the affluent. The relationship between local communities, government and global markets may be very unclear and in some cases unworkable. We need to understand the effects of globalization upon all our industries and to work together to see what kinds of individual decisions affect our most local economic environments. This is especially true in the smallest communities where diversification may be more or less impossible. A true commitment to the five marks of mission[1] means finding ways of accommodating our understanding of Christian stewardship to what is possible for these localities. We need further to know what the relationship is between pastoral concern, missionary endeavour and political and ethical consequence. We need to be aware that sometimes thinking on this is simply inadequate or hopelessly idealistic, leaving responsible and caring Christians in the same quandary as Martha and Colm.

some ideas for Bible study

Genesis 7.11-16

Matthew 4.18-22

John 21.3-14

Acts 27

questions for discussion

● How far does our understanding of global concerns about conservation and resource management affect our daily lives?

● Would you be prepared to go without for the greater good of animal or plant species, or to protect the livelihoods of others? Say why you would or would not.

● Do poverty, danger and hardship justify breaking rules? Say why they do or do not.

possibilities for drama or role play

What might it feel like to go out in a storm, labour against the force of the elements and catch nothing? How would you describe the experience to your hungry family?

Develop a biblical story of storm, such as that of Noah, Jonah, the disciples or St Paul. What sort of emotions will you feel and what difference does faith make?

Develop together a story of rescue from the storm – what does it mean to be really thankful for being saved? What kinds of 'rescue' (e.g. investment, support, more resources) could make a difference to your community?

reflection

What does God want of us as partners in sustaining and renewing our planet? What do we really mean by good stewardship and how can it be best exercised?

a hymn and a prayer

For example: 'Eternal Father, strong to save'[2] or 'Sing to God new songs of worship'[3]

> God,
> you came to the fishermen in their despair;
> you calmed the storm, you helped them cast their nets:
> give us the wisdom to hear your guiding voice,
> the faith to follow your words.
> Amen.

chapter 6
kids

Aim: to examine some rural preconceptions and attitudes about life in the city

story

A rural village community arranged to accommodate a visit from a group of primary age schoolchildren from inner-city London. The trip was intended to give city children a chance to visit a working farm, to have some exposure to the 'countryside' and a chance to meet people living in a rural environment. It was seen as a charitable (and missionary) event. It was arranged by the minister in conjunction with the church council.

At the meeting of the village church's council, the following concerns were noted:

- the church should be safeguarded against vandalism and graffiti, as it was possible the teachers would have no control over the children (and so many children all at once);
- someone would have to volunteer to be in the church to guard against possible pilfering of books etc. and against inappropriate behaviour in church (e.g. spitting and swearing);
- someone would have to provide the teachers with a list of 'don'ts' and stay with them to make sure they didn't allow the children to run riot on the farm;
- there would have to be a notice in the village newspaper about possible noise and nuisance to villagers on the day of the visit.

Another question that arose was: would there need to be translators for non-English speaking children? Another member of the church council then exhorted other members to remember that these were 'deprived' children, many without one or other parent, many black or Asian and who deserved Christian love and compassion.

The visit took place without incident and a polite letter of thanks from the children was afterwards received. The subsequent church council meeting noted that the visit had been a success and the children had so obviously benefited, another group could be invited next year. The coach was too big for country lanes and had got stuck on the bridge. The school should be asked to use minibuses instead. The children were remarkably well behaved and there had been fewer black and Asian children than expected. There were no language difficulties. It had been a good idea to have a structured programme during which the children were fully occupied. Perhaps the village should provide more food next time as the children had seemed very hungry.

discussion

In this story we can see that the rural/urban divide can be prejudiced in both directions. As a wealthy community, the rural community felt a duty to those it designated 'deprived' to share something of itself. This 'deprivation' was to be addressed as 'hospitality' and seen as a missionary endeavour. This hospitality was then to be marked by the absorption of disruption, nuisance and possibly even damage. These negative effects were discussed and publicized in advance, colouring the whole visit. There was no suggestion that the children might 'bring' anything to the village, or that anything was to be learned by encounter with them. Indeed the whole process was seen as the strong providing largesse to the weak at some cost to the ordered lives of the strong. Even after the visit had taken place and none of the worst fears had been realized, the church council still discussed what had happened in terms of problems avoided and of ministering to the deprived. The lack of problems was a pleasant (and perhaps lucky) surprise.

To reflect theologically on this, we need to look at the theology of encounter and at what missionary hospitality really means. Encounter involves risk-taking – a risk that we ourselves will be changed and challenged by the unfamiliar and the strange. Hospitality involves opening ourselves up to the unexpected and making available every part of what is ours to give. This may prove uncomfortable, especially if we already have fixed ideas about what 'others' look, sound and behave like. People shook their heads at Jesus' dining with outcasts and sinners. Those people would have been more discriminating about those to whom they offered hospitality and those from whom they would expect it. But Jesus made it clear that all kinds of preformed opinion and prejudice create obstacles for the realization of God's kingdom.

some ideas for Bible study

Genesis 18.1-8

Matthew 7.1-5

Luke 14.12-14

questions for discussion

- Where do our preconceptions come from? From newspapers, TV, cinema, things our parents said, somewhere else?
- Have you ever met someone and disliked them on sight, only to find over time that you became best of friends? What happened?
- Is it true that we sometimes know what's best for young people? Say why it is or it isn't.

possibilities for drama and role play

What would you have said to welcome the children if you were the minister? Or if you were the churchwarden, or steward?

What would the teacher have told the children to prepare them for the visit?

How do you think the teacher/children might have reported the visit back home?

reflection

We often make judgements that are ill-founded or ill-advised on the basis of what we think we know. Jesus warns us against this on several occasions. It is a mission task to approach every encounter as an occasion when God can use us to witness to the inclusiveness of the kingdom. What can we do to make this a reality?

a hymn and a prayer

For example: 'The King of love my shepherd is'[1] or 'Do not be afraid'[2]

> God,
> you welcomed children into your presence;
> you said that we must learn to be like them
> to come into your kingdom.
> May we always be your children.
> Amen.

chapter 7
old

Aim: to consider what it is like to be an elderly person in a remote area and to understand the special problems of living away from necessary facilities

story

Two elderly widows were friends and had lived in the same small rural village for years. Both were very active in the church and were considered important figures in the community. Molly was a great organizer, making sure the small congregation knew what was happening when, and was the writer, producer and deliverer of the church newsletter. Diana was known as a colourful eccentric, never afraid to say exactly what she felt about anyone to anyone. She always came to church but refused to take communion except at Christmas and at Easter. People went to Molly to find out facts about who, what, when and where. They went to Diana for uncompromising opinion about everybody, especially newcomers to church, visitors and any new arrivals in the village.

Molly could drive and regularly went into the local town to do her shopping. She was also able to visit her son and her daughter, who had moved some distance away. Although she was very mobile, she did nonetheless consider the village to be her home and the place where her roots were. Diana had never learned to drive and was heavily dependent on buying produce from the local farm and from the local shop.

The village had no bus service. When the shop closed down, and with it the sub post office, Diana took to her bicycle and cycled the eight miles to the nearest town to collect her pension and buy necessary supplies. Because she could not carry very much in her basket, she would go out every day except Sunday. She was too proud to accept a lift from anyone, or to allow people to do her shopping for her, despite many offers. Indeed, Diana on her bicycle became symbolic of the village's independent spirit.

When Molly fell ill, her son and her daughter came to visit her and both asked her to come and live with them. Molly resisted this as she felt all her roots were in the village and she did not want to leave her house. Diana then set herself to look after Molly and began to shop for both Molly and herself, carrying out double the bicycle journeys to make sure they were both provided for. Under Diana's care, Molly recovered and was very glad that she had not made the decision to sell her house and become part of her son's or daughter's household. Molly's view, however, was that it would have been easy, when she was ill, to have succumbed to the pressure to move away. The difficulties of living in an isolated village when she was ill or incapacitated, seemed to outweigh the desire to stay put in her own home.

A few years later Diana fell ill with terminal disease. As she had no family and no children, the question of how best to care for her was complicated by there being no hospital, hospice or other care facility within easy reach of her friends and neighbours. Molly, therefore, set to work to try and repay her friend's kindness, but the enormity of the task soon overwhelmed her. Diana needed specialized treatment and pain relief, and the combined efforts of all her neighbours and friends in the village were not enough to help her. Eventually, Diana had to give up her cottage, make provision for her pets, and allow herself to be moved to a hospital some distance away.

Nursing staff reported to her visitors that Diana's depression was particularly acute and difficult to treat. They noted that, beyond the progression of her disease, the removal from her community, her cottage, and her pets had created in her a sense of being dead while yet alive, so that her quality of life was reduced. Another problem was the change in the bond between herself and Molly. They had shared significant parts of their daily lives, while both were fiercely independent. They had had a common vision in which they would live out their lives in the village and die in the heart of their community. They were both distressed when that turned out to be impossible to sustain. Diana died and Molly died soon afterwards. The effect on the village was also catastrophic, with the community reeling from the loss of two of its pillars. Their strong wills and combined knowledge had been a source of inspiration for others, especially the tiny church community. Without the organizer and the voice of local opinion, gaps in the orderly process of village life opened up and the village, for a time, fell into disarray.

discussion

In today's western society we may often behave as if there were no such thing as ageing. Indeed, we are encouraged to think that we will remain young, healthy and full of possibility for ever. Yet all of us do grow older and have to make decisions about how we retain our life of independence and contribution in the face of particular needs. Such questions also may be shaped and directed by our faith and how we wish to spend our later years in serving God and building up the church. This may have to balance against the contingencies we have to prepare for: where will we live out our last years? What financial provision do we have? In the case of disability, what facilities might we lack and what difference might that make to how we can continue to live usefully?

The story illustrates some of the difficult questions elderly people can face in small rural communities. Travel and access to shopping facilities may be difficult for the elderly. Questions of where the sick can be nursed and how they can be rehabilitated after illness may be particularly acute. Lack of facilities and resources, without an adequate support network, can lead to frail and elderly people in small communities being isolated and cut off from the care they need. Pastoral care by the whole Christian community may mean more than just visiting the elderly, turning the provision of time, energy and resources into very practical help. Beyond this, too, there is the question of what the elderly in a small community can offer to the praying heart of local church life. Being disabled, sick or housebound does not mean that the elderly cannot play a full and necessary part in the missionary life of the local church. Who affirms this and sustains this expression of faith in the face of limitations is a question for the whole of any congregation to address.

suggestions for Bible study

Genesis 49.29-end

Proverbs 23.22-25

Luke 2.22-35

1 Thessalonians 5.12-22

questions for discussion

● How are elderly people supported in our village or community?

● Does anyone tend to be missed out in the network of care? If so, give examples and suggest what could be done better to help them.

● Parish Councils have the opportunity to identify the transport needs of residents and to seek solutions. How are the travel needs met in our locality?

● How are links maintained with the elderly who used to live in our village? What could we do to keep up proper links?

● Does our local church exercise an adequate visiting ministry to the elderly, including to elderly care homes?

possibilities for drama or role play

Imagine how Molly and Diana might discuss their hopes for the end part of their lives. What wishes, dreams and fears might emerge?

Imagine how Molly might discuss with her family whether she should go to live with them or stay in her own home. What sort of issues would influence the decision?

reflection

How does God want to use us as we grow older? What difference does it make to our faith and witness if we can't do as much as we used to, or would like to? What new opportunities are available to retired or elderly people to witness to faith?

a hymn and a prayer

For example: 'Abide with me; fast falls the eventide'[1] or 'I lift my eyes'[2]

> God,
> you walk with us all our lives;
> you watch us make our way towards you;
> you long to catch us when we fall.
> Help us at our end to rest in you.
> Amen.

chapter 8
young

Aim: to look at the life of young people in small communities and to understand the place of young people in the life of rural village locations

story

A young couple, Annabel and Martin, moved into a house in a small village whose population was mainly elderly, but with a few younger married couples who tended to form a club and stick together. They had met at university, where they had been firm members of the Christian Union and were deeply committed to a Bible-based Christian life. Although they were regarded (and treated) as bizarre by some of the more cynical members of the village and by some members of the church community, they persevered with church attendance and became well liked in the community. In due course they had a son, Andrew.

One day, Martin told Annabel at breakfast that he no longer loved her, had found someone else and was leaving. He moved out immediately, leaving Annabel cut off in the village with a big house and a small baby. Annabel now found herself in a complicated position in village life. First, she lost the status she had in common with other women in the village, as a mother staying at home to look after the children and taking turns to run the toddlers' club in the village hall. She had to give up her part in the social circle of the village's younger affluent couples, to consider her options. Further, she felt that her faith had crumbled away leaving only bitterness at her faithless husband and envy of the couples she still saw around her in the daily life of the village. Annabel found herself a good job to support herself and the baby, but this now meant that she had to find childcare. Offers came in from some of the retired widows in the village, but Annabel wanted a properly trained and qualified full-time nanny. This caused trouble among villagers who saw the employment of 'outsiders' as an unwelcome precedent. Annabel's first nannies found it impossible to settle in the village and none stayed long. Her life was beset by childcare problems until Andrew was old enough to go to nursery – in a town ten miles away. This left Annabel with hours in the car going back and forth to nursery and work.

As Andrew grew older, different problems appeared. With the village having rallied round Annabel and Andrew, and having cast Martin in the role of black sheep, mother and son found it difficult to throw off the shadow of 'poor relation' within the village. As Annabel began to attract new boyfriends, so people within the village treated each with extreme hostility and suspicion and acted ever more protectively towards Andrew. When Martin tried to negotiate with Annabel about where Andrew should go to school, Annabel was given a great deal of conflicting advice which made it more difficult to make sensible decisions. The village and church view was that the community wanted to 'keep' Andrew and ensure that he went to one of the local schools. Martin wanted Andrew privately educated in another part of the country.

As Andrew grew older, he began to complain that it was becoming especially difficult for him to exert any independence. Other village children went freely to other towns and villages in search of entertainment but Andrew felt he was constantly checked up on or his actions reported back. The village still seemed to have in mind that Andrew would be removed and sent away by his father. He also felt that they continued to treat him as if he were still a baby. Eventually, this sense of the village overwhelming him caused tension between Andrew and Annabel and they moved away from the village altogether.

 ## discussion

This story shows how a human tendency to categorize events and people into 'good' and 'bad' compartments can have a serious effect on people's lives. Christians who have a particularly close fellowship can be devastated and damaged when things go wrong and may overreact in the desire to make things better. In this case, the kind and sympathetic villagers tried to exercise 'ownership' of Annabel and Andrew and actually made it more difficult for her to rebuild her life and reach an accommodation with her estranged partner. On a wider basis, sometimes in tiny village communities, young people are in such a minority that they become treated as special cases and are swamped with unwelcome attention. Consequently, when the village children grow up and begin to leave for school, university or employment elsewhere their loss can be felt very acutely and even as a betrayal. The freedom to reject church, do different things, and to make mistakes can sometimes be restricted in small communities. This can lead to frustration and resentment – not just with parents, but with neighbours, friends and the whole village.

In the Church, we know that offering Christian witness to children and young people is a priority in mission. In our anxiety to reach out to a younger generation, to love, care for and to nurture them, we may forget to listen to their stories and their own accounts of their spiritual journey. Yet it is always necessary to allow others the space to encounter and be changed by the work of the Holy Spirit.

some suggestions for Bible study

2 Samuel 9

Luke 2.41-52

John 8.3-11

questions for discussion

- How do newcomers to our locality become accepted and included? Some people might have stories to share about this.
- What might have happened if Martin had been white and Annabel Afro-Caribbean?
- Forgiveness is one of Christ's commands: is this demonstrated in the life of our local church?
- Life in small communities can feel imprisoning to younger people in particular – how can they be given sufficient and appropriate freedom?

- How is childcare provided in our locality when parents are both at work? Is there more we could do to help?
- Village communities comprise wealthy and poorer people – how can they work together in community affairs?

suggestions for drama or role play

Imagine you are Annabel telling your Christian friends what has happened to your marriage and to your faith. How might they react? What would you most want to hear from them?

Imagine you are Martin coming to visit Andrew. What would you hope to hear from your Christian friends at your former church? How might they deal with your side of the story?

Put yourself in Andrew's position as he grows up. How might he explain to Annabel what he feels about life in the village?

reflection

Things can go wrong in the best Christian households, and in small communities strong emotions can prevail. How do Christian faith and fellowship help or hinder reconciliation and healing and how can all parties be helped to move on? When does our desire to love and nurture those who have been hurt become stifling?

a hymn and a prayer

For example: 'Through all the changing scenes of life'[1] or 'Born in the night'[2]

> God,
>
> you stand beside us in time of trouble;
>
> you offer us strength, courage and hope; your promises never fail:
>
> help us to have trust in your love for us,
>
> so we may turn our times of trial around.
>
> Amen.

chapter 9
grief

Aim: to look at death and bereavement in small village locations and to consider the effects of local death on small communities

story

It was at midnight on the eve of All Saints when Maggie's world fell apart.[1] Without warning her husband collapsed and died, leaving her with two small children to care for aged six and ten months. A jumble of questions ran through her mind and then continued to do so over the years. Twenty years on Maggie could see a pattern in the choices she made as a result of being a Christian in a particular rural community. At the time it felt like limping from one forced decision to another with no real choices.

The first problem was how she was going to feed the children and pay the bills. She and her husband had agreed that she wouldn't go back to work at least until the children were both in school. In a rural environment, would it be possible to honour that promise? She and her husband owned a smallholding – but how would she milk the goats, leaving the baby alone in the house while she did it? How could she bring the children up with a sense of identity with their father, without dwelling on his death too much, if she remained where she was? Would they lose the sense of identity with him if they gave everything up and moved elsewhere? How would she be able to cope with family outings to church and to other places when every other family seemed to have the father with them? How would she be able to socialize in a community that seemed to be based on couples? Feeling isolated and alone, she also wondered if she would still be and still be seen to be, a member of her husband's family.

Eventually she learned to change direction. She kept sheep instead of goats, grew all the vegetables the family needed and cut back on the work in the garden by growing shrubs instead of flowers. She kept her husband's memory alive by talking to the children about all the things they'd liked to do. She became a complete family in her widowhood. In the community in which Maggie lived, she discovered that death makes particular demands on how you reconstruct your life. She learned to dip her toe into difficult situations and withdraw quickly if it felt uncomfortable. She learned to tell people what had happened before they asked, because she couldn't cope with their embarrassment if they stumbled on the information. She learned not to look, so that she didn't notice if someone crossed the street because they felt awkward about death. She learned that the world does not feel easy about death, so she must grieve silently. She learned that if she did show her feelings, solutions were offered, but these, while well-meaning, were not always helpful. She learned that our society is often stuck in a 'couples' way of doing things and enjoying ourselves, and that this was reflected in the rural community in which she lived. However, she learned to take life seriously, filling every minute, because you never know when it will end suddenly. She learned to avoid the 'widow' and 'single parent' words because they seemed to carry a stigma. She valued the word 'family'.

Yet she also learned to recognize the grief of others and that death is part of life and cannot be avoided. She learned that grief takes a different route for everyone even though there are patterns in common. She learned to encourage her children to be positive about life, to grasp opportunities when they were offered. She was tenacious in pursuit of something even to the point of being 'a pain' if she felt the children had some kind of need she couldn't supply. She learned to value family life and that our society seems to undervalue the role of a father. She learned to question if she should provide another father for her children, but never felt that she wanted to. Maggie came to appreciate other people's successes and achievements. She learned that she had skills and achievements of her own, untapped before. She learned to admire her children for the way they have taken responsibility for their lives. She learned that life is a series of journeys. One starts as another finishes, others continue and evolve. She learned to trust in the goodness of a future.

discussion

The sudden death of spouse or partner is a traumatic experience for anyone, but this story shows how rural isolation can intensify the difficulties of recovery and rebuilding. For bereaved people like Maggie, the comfort and support of the local church can be critical in the discovery of new skills and the building up of confidence to start a new life. In this story, Maggie shows a powerful need to make sense of what has happened to her family by honouring promises made to her husband, yet she also has to find ways to adapt to the new burdens and demands placed on her by her young family.

Christian prayer and active support can either help or hinder the process of rebuilding. There is potential for a loving church community to help Maggie and her children work through the loss of a husband and father without shutting him out of their future lives. In this way, the resurrection hope shown to us in Jesus can begin to put such loss into context. Conversely, a church community which is built up around the idea of 'couples' or integrated families, can unwittingly push people like Maggie into a corner, offering sympathy and advice, but presenting her with no place in which to begin to rebuild. The local church has a real opportunity to help Maggie keep her promises to her husband and to help her find ways in which to combine work and motherhood. However, this requires a willingness to stand alongside her in her grief and to stay with her as she finds solutions to the problems. The difficulty in some churches is that the job of counselling and caring for the bereaved is left exclusively to the clergy, who may be seriously overstretched and seriously under-resourced. In such situations, the laity – neighbours and friends – can often be the only ones placed to provide the long-term support for people in Maggie's position.

some suggestions for Bible study

Psalm 68.5-10

Mark 12.41-end

1 Timothy 5.3-16

questions for discussion

- How might problems of loneliness and isolation be dealt with in rural communities?
- What facilities are available in our own church and community to help the bereaved?
- Are there fewer choices for those who are bereaved in rural locations about how they rebuild their lives?
- What is our Christian attitude in our own situation towards those people who have lost partners?

suggestions for drama or role play

Imagine you are Maggie, just after your husband's funeral, talking to a member of the clergy about how you see the future. What sort of things might you talk about? How might they respond?

Imagine you are one of Maggie's children asking questions about their father. What might Maggie say to them and what role would the support of the church have in her reply?

reflection

We need to think about what God intends for marriage and family life and further to think about what the promises people make to each other mean if a partner dies. What does God intend us to do with unfinished business and how does God encourage us to move on after tragedy and grief?

a hymn and a prayer

For example: 'The day thou gavest, Lord, is ended'[2] or 'Be still, for the presence of the Lord'[3]

> God,
> you give us life to live and celebrate;
> you know our grief when loved ones leave us:
> help us recall that you have lived through death
> and brought all loved ones home.
> Amen.

chapter 10

bed

Aim: to look at how tourism and hospitality can help to make a real difference to people's lives

story

Morag was a farmer's widow who ran a bed and breakfast facility for visitors coming to explore the countryside. With a house next to a twelfth-century church in a very rural setting, Morag hoped to offer her visitors a haven of peace, a base for refreshment and for exploring the area. Yet her Christian faith also allowed her to provide important care and witness to those coming so briefly into her home and under her care. For example, on one occasion Jenny and Derek, a couple from America, were coming to spend a holiday. Before they arrived, Morag received a telephone call at 2 a.m. from their daughter to say that Jenny's father had died and asking for them to telephone as soon as they arrived.

Jenny talked briefly of her grief but the family decided that she and Derek should stay for the week that they had planned, so the couple spent their time with Morag in the context of an unlooked-for sorrow. Jenny called in several times to the church during her stay and one day came to Morag and said that she had woven a wreath out of the hips she had gathered from the hedgerows and had placed it in the church. She asked Morag if anyone would mind. On the last day of their stay it was Harvest Festival and Morag agreed with the people decorating the church that the appropriate place for Jenny's wreath was on the cross. Later, having heard Jenny's story and knowing that the hips would dry and last a long time, everyone in the church community decided to leave it in place when the rest of the decorations were taken down.

Jenny and Derek joined the community for the service and were very moved that Jenny's wreath had been placed on the cross. In praising God, there was opportunity to remember and give thanks for all the good things about the countryside and the need to nurture the fruits of the earth. This went alongside the need for everyone to give thanks for the lives of all those we love. The congregation remembered the suffering in the rural community and this related directly to the suffering of anyone who loses something or someone they love. Jenny afterwards affirmed not only how much she had enjoyed the service and had been comforted by it, but how she would love to support a church community like Morag's. In doing so, she affirmed both Morag's own ministry as one who understood her grief, but also the role of the small rural church in being a centre for mission, healing and refreshment. This was true, not only for the local community, but for travellers from all over the world. In making the link between those staying for bed and breakfast and her local church, Morag provided a vital witness and ministry.

discussion

Walkers, casual visitors and tourists are a significant part of the life of rural Britain and bring much needed resources into remote parts of the country. Such visitors also frequently visit churches in the countryside. Those Christians engaged in providing food and accommodation have a particular opportunity to offer a witness to their faith, and hospitality may make a great difference to people staying for a brief time. Morag's story shows particularly how she was placed to make a link for Jenny to the local church, which provided Jenny with the context for expressing her grief. Yet Morag had to gain Jenny's trust and create a relationship in which the wreath of hips could become a potent symbol of resurrection hope.

Churches too have special opportunities to witness to tourists and visitors, but in remote locations there are often difficult questions about whether it is safe or proper to leave churches open and unattended. Questions of access are sometimes hard to solve. Some villages find it hard to believe that their local church has anything much to offer visitors if the building is not of great historic interest or possessed of a wealth of unusual features. Sometimes the missionary potential of a modest flower festival, or display of children's paintings is overlooked.

Holidaymakers may be in a better position than others to engage in reflection. A quiet wander into a church may just provide the beginning of a questioning and taking stock to which a sympathetic Christian presence may make all the difference. In Jenny's case, Morag's help and encouragement were exactly what was needed.

some suggestions for Bible study

Leviticus 19.33

Luke 10.38-end

Hebrews 13.2

questions for discussion

- What opportunities for hospitality are there in our own situation? Do we make the best use of these opportunities?
- What does our local church offer to visitors? How can our church building be helped to speak of God's love for all?
- What events take place that could be acts of witness? How could they be made more effective and attractive?
- What use can we, or do we, make of our own homes to offer people hospitality?

suggestions for drama or role play

Imagine you are Morag welcoming Jenny and Derek into your home. How would you break it to them that they must phone home?

Try making wreaths from natural materials. What does it mean to place your wreath on the cross?

Imagine you are decorating the church for harvest festival. What might you tell a visitor about what you are doing and why?

reflection

Through our hospitality towards others, God gives us particular opportunities to witness to our faith through both being and doing. How do we extend a ministry of hospitality to all those we encounter?

a hymn and a prayer

For example: 'We plough the fields and scatter'[1] or 'Come, you thankful people, come'[2]

God,
you are the source of all our harvests;
you are the provider of all good gifts:
may we always show others the gift of your love.
Amen.

chapter 11

hope

Aim: to look for the sources of Christian hope in times of great change and affliction in the countryside

story

James and Annie had farmed the 120 acres of Long Meadow Farm for thirty years. They had only taken over fully when James's father died. They raised beef cattle and sheep, feeding them almost completely from what was grown on the farm. In James's family, farming had always been considered a good living and farming had been their life for three generations before James was born. Annie came from the nearby market town and had settled into the farming way of life.

They rented 120 acres and in good times had bought a further 60 acres a few miles away. But with BSE, the high value of the pound and then the onset of foot-and-mouth disease, the farm began to return insufficient amounts to pay the bills. In a short time, James had accumulated a debt that could not be cleared. As a tenant, the bank would not give him any more help. Annie had to take a part-time job in the town to keep the farm's finances afloat. This nearly came to grief, however, when the businesses started to close in the wake of foot-and-mouth. The hotels laid off staff and the petrol station closed down, leaving Annie with the worry that her own job, related to tourist services, would be next to go. Despite their struggle, James and Annie had to face the reality that neither of their two sons, or their daughter would want to take on the farm when they retired, and that all of them lived over 30 miles away.

James began to have nightmares about foot-and-mouth disease affecting his animals. The fear of the disease scarred him deeply and led to trouble when he refused to allow walkers on to footpaths around his land, despite the countryside being declared 'open'. The tourists and walkers were unsympathetic to the fact that James cared for and knew each of his animals, each of which would be sent to slaughter with a tear in James's eye. They simply saw him as being paranoid and unhelpful.

James's father had been an officer of the local church for 20 years, but James lost so much confidence that he lost contact with the church and with many of his friends. Annie stayed on both the church council and the Women's Institute. Although foot-and-mouth did not come to their farm, the movement restrictions made life impossible and James felt he had hit an all-time low when he had to put his pride aside and ask for help from the Royal Agricultural Benevolent Institution and from the ARC Addington Fund[1]. He was put in touch with one of the agricultural chaplains, a layperson who had once been a farmer himself.

The chaplain came out to visit James and Annie several times, and talked through the possibility of giving up the farm. Through him, James also talked to the Farm Business Advisory Service. The chaplain encouraged James to see how many skills he had as a practical farmer, so that starting something new was a way of using those talents, not giving up. James had to learn to get past the idea of the farm as an inherited obligation and find change a positive step, releasing him from the appalling stress. The chaplain also helped James begin to think about alternative accommodation and offered to help him talk to the estate about his options.

discussion

This story has many strands that have been repeated many times during the foot-and-mouth crisis. The disease does not just affect farmers, but all kinds of businesses and industries in local economies. This shows the interdependence of various kinds of infrastructure and how people's livelihoods are connected. Things can go badly wrong where interests clash in the process of self-protection as can be seen in the clash of interests between the farm and the tourist industry. The difficulty is in turning a personal tragedy into a set of possibilities out of which hope can come.

The Church should be the place to which Christians turn for the articulation of hope, but sometimes we are ill equipped to deal with the loss of confidence and blows to faith that come with adversity. Sometimes we find it even more difficult to stand beside people who find themselves in adversity; we start to treat them differently or revise our friendships in subtle ways. Yet Jesus insists that we work hard always to treat our neighbours as ourselves, no matter whether they can offer us little or much in return.

some suggestions for Bible study

Job 1.1-11

Isaiah 10.18-27

John 3.1-10

questions for discussion

- What might it feel like to have to give up a business for which you have worked so hard?
- How would you feel if you were in James's shoes?
- What view might Annie take about leaving the farm after 30 years?
- How might local church people help James?
- What attitude could the estate take towards helping a tenant who can't pay rent?
- What is the future for the estate with such a loss of rental income?
- What will happen to the community if the estate fails?

suggestions for drama or role play

What might James say to Annie at the point where he realized he could not go on farming?

What might they both say to the farm workers, people in the church, the community?

44

Imagine the discussions between the chaplain and James. What sort of things might they talk about?

Imagine the discussion between James, the chaplain and an estate representative. How will they decide what to do for the best?

reflection

Sometimes it is very difficult to make sense of calamity and disaster in terms of God's plan for the whole creation. Sometimes Christians opt for simple moralizing or for bafflingly complex ways of trying to make sense of such situations, which leave people feeling rejected or confused. Yet God promises us that there is always the possibility of creating something new out of adversity. How can we witness to the eternal nature of Christian hope and how can we help to make it a reality in people's lives?

a hymn and a prayer

For example: 'All my hope on God is founded'[2] or 'The light of Christ'[3]

God,
the world is not always kind,
things do not turn out as we would wish or desire,
but you hold out your hand in good times and bad,
offering us new dreams and eternal hope.
Amen.

references

All the following titles are published by ACORA Publishing, The Arthur Rank Centre, National Agricultural Centre, Stoneleigh Park, Warwickshire, CV8 2LZ, telephone 024 7685 8347. The Arthur Rank Centre is the main point of contact for all matters concerning rural churches.

books

David Gatward, *See You Down the Bus Shelter*, 2001
A report on the process and benefits of the small grant scheme for rural church youth work administered through the Arthur Rank Centre.

Elfrida Savigear, *The Servant Church*, 1996
A realistic book on church-initiated schemes of care in rural community, giving practical advice on such matters as insurance, supervision of volunteers, prayer support and finance.

Leslie Francis and Jeremy Martineau, *Rural Praise*, 1996
This book aims to help church groups think through their worship needs in the light of many choices and a variety of preferences.

Leslie Francis and Jeremy Martineau, *Rural Visitors*, 2001
A parish workbook for welcoming visitors to the country church.

Leslie Francis and Jeremy Martineau, *Rural Youth*, 2001
An easy-to-use, vital tool for anyone working with young people in schools, churches and the community in general.

Leslie Francis, Keith Littler and Jeremy Martineau,
Rural Ministry, 2000
A parish workbook offering the opportunity to develop the commitment of lay people to ministry in the church and community.

Mike Alexander and Jeremy Martineau, *So the Vicar's Leaving*, 2nd edition, 2001
The standard guidance book for local church leaders considering or facing an interregnum.

Jeremy Martineau (ed.), *Bridging the Gap*, 1999
A short workbook for churches examining their relationship with the local community. It can be used as a basis for local mission.

Jeremy Martineau (ed.), *Turning the Sod*, 1995
A workbook designed for Anglican church groups considering the possibilities presented by several parishes sharing a minister.

John Brown, *Celebrating the Rural Church*, 2001
A report on progress in key areas of church activity, ten years on from *Faith in the Countryside*.

Susan Rowe, *Open All Hours*, 2001
This book draws on the experience of the Rural Churches in Community Service programme in adapting 100 churches to meet contemporary community needs.

periodical

Country Way, published three times a year
A colour magazine full of ideas, information and inspiration, now established as the specialist magazine for rural Christian thinking and practice.

notes

chapter 1 food
1. 'Guide me, O thou great Redeemer', *Hymns Ancient and Modern New Standard*, Hymns Ancient and Modern Limited, 1983.
2. 'We come as guests invited', *Mission Praise*, Marshall Pickering, 1990.

chapter 2 dark
1. See Ronald Blyth's essay on 'dark' in the *Church Times*, 10 December 1999.
2. 'Lead, kindly Light', *Hymns Ancient and Modern New Standard*, Hymns Ancient and Modern Limited, 1983.
3. 'Like a candle flame', *Mission Praise*, Marshall Pickering, 1990.

chapter 3 pub
1. 'City of God, how broad and far', *Hymns Ancient and Modern New Standard*, Hymns Ancient and Modern Limited, 1983.
2. 'Jesus put this song into our hearts', *Mission Praise*, Marshall Pickering, 1990.

chapter 4 grave
1. Wink, Walter, *Naming the Powers*, Fortress Press, 1984; *Unmasking the Powers*, Fortress Press, 1986; *Engaging the Powers*, Fortress Press, 1992.
2. 'God is working his purpose out', *Hymns Ancient and Modern Revised*, Hymns Ancient and Modern Limited, 1981.
3. 'How lovely is thy dwelling-place', *Mission Praise*, Marshall Pickering, 1990.

chapter 5 fish
1. The five marks of mission have their provenance from *The truth shall make you free*, Church House Publishing, 1988 (a report of the 1988 Lambeth Conference). The five marks are: to proclaim the good news of the kingdom; to teach, baptize and nurture new believers; to respond to human need by loving service; to seek to transform unjust structures of society; to strive to safeguard the integrity of creation and sustain and renew the earth.
2. 'Eternal Father, strong to save', *Hymns Ancient and Modern New Standard*, Hymns Ancient and Modern Limited, 1983.
3. 'Sing to God new songs of worship', *Mission Praise*, Marshall Pickering, 1990.

chapter 6 kids
1. 'The King of love my shepherd is', *Hymns Ancient and Modern New Standard*, Hymns Ancient and Modern Limited, 1983.
2. 'Do not be afraid', *Mission Praise*, Marshall Pickering, 1990.

chapter 7   old

1. 'Abide with me; fast falls the eventide', *Hymns Ancient and Modern New Standard*, Hymns Ancient and Modern Limited, 1983.

2. 'I lift my eyes', *Mission Praise*, Marshall Pickering, 1990.

chapter 8   young

1. 'Through all the changing scenes of life', *Hymns Ancient and Modern New Standard*, Hymns Ancient and Modern Limited, 1983.

2. 'Born in the night', *Mission Praise*, Marshall Pickering, 1990.

chapter 9   grief

1. A version of this story was published anonymously in *Stories from the Chronicles*, Volume 2, Marches Chronicles, May 2000.

2. 'The day thou gavest, Lord, is ended', *Hymns Ancient and Modern New Standard*, Hymns Ancient and Modern Limited, 1983.

3. 'Be still, for the presence of the Lord', *Mission Praise*, Marshall Pickering, 1990.

chapter 10   bed

1. 'We plough the fields and scatter', *Hymns Ancient and Modern New Standard*, Hymns Ancient and Modern Limited, 1983.

2. 'Come, you thankful people, come', *Mission Praise*, Marshall Pickering, 1990.

chapter 11   hope

1. This fund is administered through the Arthur Rank Centre (ARC), National Agricultural Centre, Stoneleigh Park, Warks, CV8 2LZ.

2. 'All my hope on God is founded', *Hymns Ancient and Modern New Standard*, Hymns Ancient and Modern Limited, 1983.

3. 'The light of Christ', *Mission Praise*, Marshall Pickering, 1990.

index